Eggs for Breakfast

By JOwen

Library For All Ltd.

Eggs for Breakfast

First published 2022

Published by Library For All Ltd
Email: info@libraryforall.org
URL: libraryforall.org

Our Yarning logo design by Jason Lee, Bidjipidji Art

Original illustrations by Fariza Dzatalin Nurtsani

Eggs for Breakfast
JOwen
ISBN: 978-1-922835-72-7
SKU01401

Eggs for Breakfast

We respect and honour Aboriginal and Torres Strait Islander Elders past, present and future. We acknowledge the stories, traditions and living cultures of Aboriginal and Torres Strait Islander peoples on this land and commit to building a brighter future together.

Good morning! I'm hungry.

What do you like to eat
for breakfast?

I like eggs and toast.
Here's how I make it.

Take an egg and put it in a small saucepan of cold water.

Be gentle so it doesn't crack!

Put the saucepan on the stove and turn it up to 'hot'.

You might need an adult to help for this part.

When the water starts boiling, wait for 5 minutes.

Can you see a clock?

Can you see the egg bouncing in the bubbles?

While you wait, you can put some bread in the toaster and get your butter ready.

Put your plate, egg cup, knife, and spoon on the table.

5 minutes! Well done
for waiting.

Now, use a big spoon
to scoop the egg out of
the water. Don't burn
your fingers.

Pop! The toast is ready.

Spread some butter on it and cut it into three strips.

Are you thirsty too?

Pour a glass of milk or juice
to enjoy with your meal.

Now, cut the top off your egg carefully with your knife.

You can dip your toast into the gooey egg. Yum!

You've made a
healthy breakfast.

You'll have lots of energy
now to play and learn.

Wait!

Don't forget to clean
up after yourself!

You can use these questions to talk about this book with your family, friends and teachers.

What did you learn from this book?

Describe this book in one word. Funny? Scary? Colourful? Interesting?

How did this book make you feel when you finished reading it?

What was your favourite part of this book?

download our reader app
getlibraryforall.org

About the author

JOwen is from the Nurrunga/Ngarrindjeri Nations of South Australia. She was born in Adelaide and now lives in Broome, Western Australia. She loves the laughs and fun of family gatherings. As a child her favourite book was *I Can Jump Puddles*.

Our Yarning

Want to discover more books from this collection? Our Yarning is a collection of books written by Aboriginal and Torres Strait Islander peoples across Australia.

We know that children learn better, and enjoy reading more, when they see themselves in the stories, characters and illustrations of the books they read.

To download the app, visit the Google Play Store on any Android device and search 'Our Yarning'.

www.ingramcontent.com/pod-product-compliance
Lightning Source LLC
Chambersburg PA
CBHW042342040426
42448CB00019B/3372